Tw

Faux Fur Fun

Alistair Macdonald

Search Press

First published in 2015

Search Press Limited
Wellwood, North Farm Road,
Tunbridge Wells, Kent TN2 3DR

Text copyright © Alistair Macdonald 2015

Photographs by Paul Bricknell at
Search Press Studios

Photographs and design copyright
© Search Press Ltd 2015

Print ISBN: 978-1-78221-202-7
ebook ISBN: 978-1-78126-262-7

The Publishers and author can accept no
responsibility for any consequences arising from
the information, advice or instructions given in
this publication.

Readers are permitted to reproduce any of
the items in this book for their personal use,
or for the purposes of selling for charity,
free of charge and without the prior
permission of the Publishers. Any use of the
items for commercial purposes is not
permitted without the prior permission of
the Publishers.

Suppliers
If you have difficulty in obtaining any of the
materials and equipment mentioned in this
book, then please visit the Search Press
website for details of suppliers:
www.searchpress.com

Printed in China

Dedication
*I would like to dedicate this book
to my 'wee' son, T S-M.*

Contents

Introduction

Faux fur has certainly moved on since the days when it was considered a child's craft fabric, and definitely not at all realistic. By today's standards, faux fur is a luxurious, high-tech and extremely realistic material to work with. Often, I find myself having to get really close to make a careful assessment of its origins. Boasting a huge array of animal prints, colour, style and, more importantly, movement, faux fur has become a 'go to' fabric, rather than one to avoid.

But what to do with this amazing textile and how to handle it? Fear not! With this *Twenty to Make*, I will teach you how, and share with you the secrets I have learned in the fashion industry. With a little practice, you will soon be producing outstanding furry creations.

In this book you will find something for everyone. Add some Hollywood glamour with a wrap that Marilyn Monroe would have been proud of, trim a bag and gloves for some furry *je ne sais quoi*, add an eye-poppingly stylish fur collar to a jacket – or simply let your wild side out and bring a monster beanbag to life in your home.

All of the designs are easy to follow and come with step-by-step instructions, as well as diagrams and measurements to help you plot out templates. You do not have to be a professional – just have a love of all things furry.

Let the fur games begin, and get sewing!

Techniques

Attaching the lining/bias tape

Attaching lining/bias tape not only allows you to finish the raw edges of fur, but it also helps give the fur 'body' and the feeling of fullness. The process stabilises the outer edges and means you do not need to use an iron (which should never be used on fur, whether it be real or faux). This technique is used throughout the projects found within this book.

The tape should always be sewn directly onto the fur side to avoid puckering. When attaching the tape, comb any stray fur inwards under the tape while you sew. This prevents the fur becoming trapped within the seam, which will look ugly when the tape has been 'rolled' to the reverse of the fur (see below). The back of the blades of a pair of dressmaking snips are an ideal tool to comb back the fur.

'Rolling' the fur

'Rolling' the fur is a very important technique. After the lining/bias tape has been attached, roll the tape towards the reverse side of the fur. As your thumb folds the tape over, gently roll a little of the fur edge with the tape. Baste the tape to the fur backing with a running stitch 1cm (½in) away from the seam. This will achieve a plumper edge and prevent the fur from looking flat.

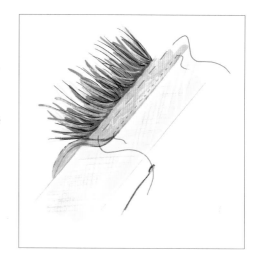

Machine stitching sizes

Many of the projects within this book include instructions to machine stitch part of the project using a 'large stitch'. Please note that a large stitch equates to UK stitch size 4 –5 (US stitch size 6–5).

Cutting faux fur

Always use a scalpel to cut fur and never scissors. If you use scissors, you will end up cutting the long fibres off. Always cut on the reverse side of the fur.

As you cut with the knife, use your other hand to hold the fur above the knife. Use your fingers to gently pull the cut line apart (see below). Holding the work in this way is also important to counteract the drag or pull that a knife produces. Using a knife also reduces the amount of loose fur produced during the cutting process.

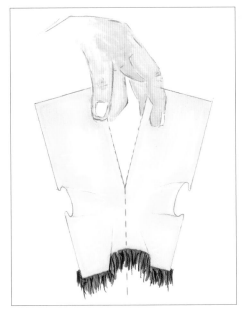

Hair direction and pile consideration

As a general rule, fur should always face or point down towards the ground. If the hair has a much shorter pile, this rule can be reversed because it will give the illusion that the colour of the fur is deeper and more intense (rather like using velvet).

As fur is similar to hair and varies in length, this needs to be considered when plotting out a pattern or template. If you wish the fur to stop at a certain depth or level, you will need to deduct the hair length from the base of a pattern. This is where the hair will naturally overhang. If you do not do this, you will end up with a much deeper trim.

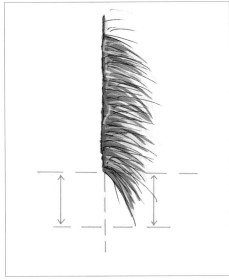

Working with animal markings

Some furs have animal markings, which need to be taken into consideration when placing pattern pieces so that symmetry can be achieved. If you are lucky, the markings will be visible on the reverse. Where this is not the case, try using large quilting pins to show this. Insert the pins from the fur side, placing them along any markings, towards the reverse of the fur piece, and chalk along the pins to transfer the information. Repeat as necessary.

Glove Trim

Materials:

- 2 x faux silver fox fur strips approx. 5 x 20cm (2 x 7¾in)
- 0.5m (19¾in) of lining fabric
- One pair of gloves

Tools:

Fabric scissors

Scalpel

Thread

Sewing machine

Hand sewing needles

Chalk/pencil

Iron

Long, strong pins

Ruler and tape measure

Instructions:

1 Start by taking a few basic measurements from the gloves you wish to trim: the circumference of the opening and the depth of the fur from the top of the glove down to where the fur will end. My measurements for these red leather gloves are 20cm (7¾in) round the wrist and a depth of 7.5cm (3in). Use these measurements to mark directly onto the fabric side of the fur. Remember to subtract the hair length from the depth measurement. For this project, I have used a faux silver fox fur and the hair length is 2.5cm (1in), therefore my chalked pattern should now measure 5cm (2in) to obtain a finished depth of 7.5cm (3in). Add 5mm (¼in) round the entire piece as a seam allowance.

2 With the patterns chalked out, make sure the direction of the fur is running from top to bottom and carefully cut out using a knife. Bring the short ends of each section together and pin to secure. Machine stitch 5mm (¼in)

away from the raw edge using a large stitch. As you stitch, comb any fur towards the centre of the piece (see page 6). You should have two tube-like cuffs.

3 Lay the lining flat and chalk out some bias strips 8cm (3¼in) wide and approximately 10cm (4in) longer than the circumference measurement. You will need two strips per cuff. Cut these out. Press each piece in half along the longest edge. Take each cuff and pin the folded bias edge to the raw edge of the fur. Overlap the bias strip back on itself at the starting point. This will achieve a nice finished edge when 'rolling' the fur. Repeat this on all four sides.

4 Machine stitch using a large stitch along the pinned edges, combing any fur to the centre. As you reach the beginning of the stitch line, overlap the bias tape by approximately 4cm (1½in). Cut off any excess tape. To complete each cuff, 'roll' the fur by folding the bias tape towards the fabric side of the fur and hand sew it into position (see page 6).

5 To attach each cuff to a glove, first turn the glove inside out and insert the cuff into the glove. Make sure the seam line of the fur is positioned to the underside of the glove (the fur direction should be pointing down into the glove). Hand stitch the rim of the glove to the rim of the cuff to secure. Turn the whole piece through to the right side.

Boot Cuffs

Materials:

Faux silver fox fur

0.5m (19¾in) of lining fabric

One pair of boots

Tools:

Fabric scissors

Scalpel

Threads

Sewing machine

Hand sewing needles

Chalk/pencil

Iron

Long, strong pins

Ruler and tape measure

Pattern paper

Instructions:

1 First, you will need to make a pattern using the boots you wish to trim. Lay one of your boot tops flat onto some pattern paper with the inside leg facing down onto the paper. Draw round the top of the boot and down each side. Remove the boot and neaten the lines. Measure down to the desired depth for the finished trim, taking into account the hair length of the faux fur you have chosen. Draw in the line and mark this piece as 'front'. Repeat this process for the inside leg of the boot by turning the boot over. Once this second piece is drawn, cut out and fold it in half (from left to right). Cut along the fold line. Matching the sides of the pattern pieces, add one to either side of the piece marked 'front'. Stick down with tape to secure. Using the bottom line of the 'front' piece, level the bottom of the newly joined side pieces. This will position the join of the fur to the centre of the inside leg, once constructed.

2 Lay this pattern onto the fabric side of the faux fur and chalk out two sections, one for each boot. Add 5mm (¼in) seam allowance round all edges and cut out using a scalpel. Before cutting, check that the fur direction is running from top to bottom. Bring the short edges of each piece together and pin to secure. Machine stitch 5mm (¼in) away from the raw edge using a large stitch. Always stitch

the tape onto the fur to avoid puckering. As you stitch, comb any fur towards the centre of the piece (see page 6).

3 Mark out four bias strips from the lining material, each 8cm (3¼in) wide and long enough to trim round the outside edges of the fur boot cuffs, and cut out. Press each piece in half along the longest edge. Take each cuff and pin the folded bias edge to the raw edge of the fur on the bottom sections only. For the top sections match all of the raw edges, allowing the pressed fold line to point away from the raw edge. Overlap each bias strip back on itself at the starting point. This will achieve a nice finished edge when 'rolling' the fur. Repeat on all four sides. Machine stitch to secure, as for step 2.

4 'Roll' the fur along the bottom edge of each cuff by folding the bias tape towards the fabric side of the fur and hand sew into position (see page 6). Now place each cuff over the outside of a boot and line up the inside leg seam. Once in place, match the top of the cuff with the rim of the boot and fold the bias tape over and pin to the inside of the boot. After pinning, hand sew along the pressed edge of the tape to secure. Repeat this process for the second boot.

Fur-trimmed Bag

Materials:

Faux silver fox and
  racoon fur

0.5m (19¾in) of lining fabric

One bag

Keyring chain

Tools:

Fabric scissors

Scalpel

Thread

Sewing machine

Hand sewing needles

Chalk/pencil

Iron

Long, strong pins

Ruler and tape measure

Pattern paper

Instructions:

1 First, take some measurements of the bag
you wish to trim: the circumference of the
base and an intended depth for the racoon fur
trim, taking the fur length into account. Mark
these measurements straight onto the fabric
side of the faux fur. It is best to divide the
circumference measurement in half to produce
two sections. This will give you equal joins in
the fur to align either side of the bag. Add
5mm (¼in) seam allowance round all edges and
cut out using a scalpel.

2 Now turn to page 8 and follow steps 2–4 of
the Glove Trim project. You will need only two
strips of bias tape and, essentially, you are only
making one big 'cuff'.

3 Once the trim is at this stage, place it over
the bag with the fur running from top to
bottom. Line up the joins with each bag side
and in the centre. Hand stitch the trim to the
base of the bag with a sharp needle. Now fill
the bag to pad it out. This will make it much
easier to stitch the top of the trim to the bag.

4 To make the fox tail bag charm, draw out the
following pattern onto some pattern paper. Use
the measurements and the diagram to help
you plot the following: 0–1 = 20cm (7¾in), 1–2
= 2cm (¾in), 1–5 = 2cm (¾in), 0–3 = 5cm (2in),
0–4 = 5cm (2in). Join 4–5 and 3–2 with a curved
line as shown. Cut out the pattern and use to

mark out one tail onto the fabric side of the
faux fur. Cut the tail out using the scalpel. Bring
the curved edges together with the right sides
facing and secure with pins. Machine stitch
5mm (¼in) away from the raw edge using a
large stitch, combing any fur towards the
centre of the piece.

5 Turn the fox tail through to expose the long
hair. Hand stitch the top of the tail closed and
attach the keyring. There is no need to close
the bottom edge of the tail as this is hidden by
the long fur hanging down.

6 Clip the keyring to the bag.

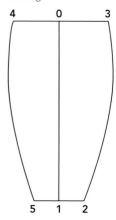

*Pattern
(not to scale)*

Pompom Clutch Bag

Materials:

Faux chinchilla fur

0.5m (19¾in) of
    lining fabric

0.5m (19¾in) of fabric
    for the purse outer
    (I have used a
    black Melton)

2 x Styrofoam® balls
    4cm (1½in)
    in diameter

1 x snap fastener

Tools:

Fabric scissors

Scalpel

Threads (strong and normal)

Sewing machine

Hand sewing needles

Chalk/pencil

Long strong pins

Ruler and tape measure

4 x sheets of paper, 210 x
    297mm (8¼ x 11¾in)

Sticky tape

Compasses

Instructions:

1 Set compasses to 7cm (2¾in) and draw a circle onto a sheet of paper. This is the template for the pompoms. Cut out the circle and set aside. Join the three remaining sheets in a landscape format with sticky tape (one beneath the other). Fold the bottom sheet in half from bottom to top, longways and cut along the fold line. Discard the loose piece of paper. On the remaining half, mark the centre of the paper and draw a semicircular line from one corner to the centre. Mirror exactly on the opposite side. Trim along this curved line. Your pattern should look like the diagram (right).

2 Use the pattern to mark out one full shape onto the fabric. Use scissors to cut off the semicircular part of the pattern. This pattern piece will form a lining for the flap of the bag. Mark out this new shape. Cut both pieces out. Use the remaining pattern piece to mark out and cut out the other lining. Pin the two curved edges together and machine stitch them closed 1cm (½in) away from the raw edge. Trim the seam allowance 5mm (¼in) away from this stitch line and turn through. Top stitch the curve 1cm (½in) away from the outside edge. Turn over 1cm (½in) along the opposite end from the flap and topstitch down. Now with right sides facing, fold the bag in half until the flat edge meets the fold line of the flap. Pin the sides, machine close and turn through.

3 Fold the lining section in half with right sides facing, pin and machine close down the short sides only. Now drop this lining into the bag and pin into position, turning 1cm (½in) along the raw edge for a neat finish. Hand stitch into position. Mark the desired position of the snap fastening and attach.

4 To make the pompoms mark out two circles using the template and chalk. Cut out using a scalpel. With a very strong thread, apply a running stitch round the perimeter of each circle 5mm (¼in) away from the raw edge, leaving the thread ends free. Draw both threads together at the same time to encase a polystyrene ball. This will form a pompom. Tie a series of knots to secure the fur round the ball tightly. Using the remaining threads, sew the pompoms onto the bag in the desired position.

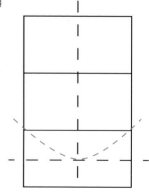

*Pattern
(not to scale)*

14

Slide-through Scarf

Materials:
Faux chinchilla fur

1m (39½in) of lining fabric

Tools:
Fabric scissors

Scalpel

Thread

Sewing machine

Hand sewing needles

Chalk/pencil

Long, strong pins

Ruler and tape measure

Pattern paper

Iron

Instructions:

1 Mark out a rectangle measuring 109 x 17cm (43 x 6¾in) onto the pattern paper and cut out. Fold the rectangle in half lengthways to find the middle. With a pencil, mark a 15cm (6in) line for the slide-through opening 21cm (8¼in) away from one of the shorter ends. Unfold the paper and mark a welt (traditionally used when making a pocket opening). Create a 2cm (¾in) box the same length as your pencil line, making sure the crease line runs through the middle. Mark in the cutting lines shown in the diagram (right).

2 Divide the pattern in two and cut along the fold line. From these newly cut lines, mark arrows pointing away to indicate fur direction. This will ensure that both sides of the scarf will fall in the same direction, rather than one pointing down and the other up. Place the pattern pieces onto the fabric side of the fur and mark with chalk, transferring all the information. Add a 5mm (¼in) seam allowance round the pieces and cut out with a scalpel. Cut a piece of lining measuring 25 x 10cm (9¾ x 4in). Pin this section onto the fur side, covering the area where the welt is to be created. With a sewing machine, stitch round the marked welt with a large stitch. This will attach the lining to the fur. With scissors, cut through both fur and lining, following the cutting lines. Pull the lining through the hole and pin onto the fabric side of the fur. Stitch into place and remove the pins to finish the opening.

3 Bring the two fur sections together to form the centre seam of the scarf and pin. The fur should be running away from the centre. Machine sew the pieces together 5mm (¼in) away from the raw edge using a large stitch.

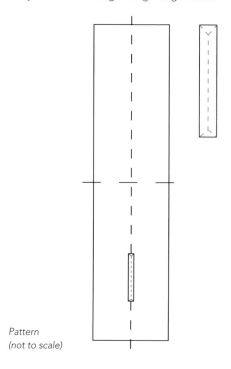

Pattern
(not to scale)

4 Lay the lining flat and chalk out some bias strips 8cm wide and about 260cm long (3¼ x 102¼in). Cut out and join the strips together with a sewing machine. Press in half along the longest edge. Turn the scarf fur side up and pin the folded bias edge to the raw edge of the fur (start at the centre seam). Overlap the bias strip back on itself at the starting point. This will achieve a nice finished edge when 'rolling' the fur. Repeat on all sides.

5 Machine stitch in a large stitch size along the pinned edges, combing any fur to the centre. As you reach the beginning of the stitch line, overlap the bias tape by about 4cm (1½in). Cut off any excess tape. Now 'roll' the fur by folding the bias tape towards the fabric side of the fur and hand sew into position (see page 6).

6 Chalk out a lining as one piece, marking the welt size and position. Add an extra 2cm (¾in) seam allowance round the whole lining piece and cut out. With scissors, cut through the cutting lines of the welt. Press the welt open with an iron towards the wrong side. Offer the pressed welt over the scarf welt and pin. Now tuck under the raw edges of the lining round the perimeter and pin onto the bias tape 5mm (¼in) away from the edge. Take care when folding under the corners so as not to make the lining tight. Hand sew the lining into position to finish the scarf and remove the pins.

Hollywood Wrap

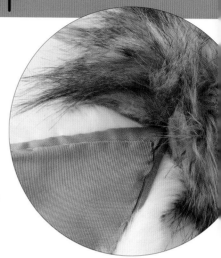

Materials:

Faux white rabbit fur (panelled) and a small amount of faux racoon fur for pompoms

2m (78¾in) of lining fabric

2 x polystyrene balls 5cm (2in) in diameter

Tools:

Fabric scissors

Scalpel

Thread (strong and normal)

Sewing machine

Hand sewing needles

Chalk/pencil

Long, strong pins

Ruler and tape measure

Pattern paper

Iron

Compasses

Instructions:

1 Take a piece of pattern paper approximately 50 x 100cm (19¾ x 39½in). Fold in half to create a piece now measuring 25 x 100cm (9¾ x 39½in). With the fold at the bottom, mark 20cm (7¾in) up on the left hand side. Now, mark the following along the fold (from left to right): 30cm/11¾in (at this point also mark 18cm/7in vertically above), 50cm/19¾in (11cm/4¼in vertically above) and 83cm/32¾in (7cm/2¾in vertically above). The vertical points are to guide you when creating the curved lines of the pattern. Now join up the vertical points with a pencil and, once you are happy with the curves, cut along the pencil line. Unfold the paper to reveal a half pattern for the wrap. The straight line of the pattern is the centre seam.

2 Use this pattern to chalk out two sections onto the fabric side of the fur. Pay attention to fur direction and left-/right-hand sections. Cut out the two sections with a scalpel.

3 Bring the two fur sections together to form the centre seam of the wrap and pin. The fur should be running parallel with the centre seam. Machine sew the pieces together 5mm (¼in) away from the raw edge using a large stitch. Now follow steps 4 and 5 of the Slide-through Scarf on page 17. You will need to measure round the scarf to determine how much tape you will need.

4 Chalk out a lining as one piece, using the paper pattern, and mark the centre seam position. If your lining is not wide enough, you will need to cut two sections and stitch them together before application. Add an extra 2cm (¾in) seam allowance round the whole lining piece and cut out. Turn the whole wrap flat fur side down. Place the lining over the wrap and match up the centre seam markings and the scarf tips. Pin to hold. Now tuck under the raw edges of the lining round the perimeter and pin onto the bias tape 5mm (¼in) away from the edge. Take care when folding under the corners so as not to pull the lining tight. Hand sew the lining into position and remove the pins.

5 Set compasses to 8.5cm (3³/₈in), draw a circle onto pattern paper and cut out your template. To make the pompoms, mark two circles with chalk onto the dark faux fur using the circle template. Cut out using a scalpel. With a very strong thread, apply a running stitch round the perimeter of each circle 5mm (¼in) away from the raw edge, leaving the thread ends free. Place a polystyrene ball in the centre of the fur and draw both threads together to encase the ball and form a pompom. Tie a series of knots to secure the fur tightly round the polystyrene ball. Using the remaining threads, sew a pompom to each end of the wrap.

Hot Water Bottle Cover

Materials:

Faux white tiger-printed rabbit fur

0.5m (19¾in) of lining fabric

5 x 100cm (2 x 39½in) of black satin ribbon

1.5 x 15cm (⁵/₈in x 6in) of black grosgrain ribbon

One hot water bottle

Tools:

Fabric scissors

Scalpel

Thread

Sewing machine

Hand sewing needles

Chalk/pencil

Long, strong pins

Ruler and tape measure

Pattern paper

Iron

Instructions:

1 Make a pattern for your chosen hot water bottle. Lay out some pattern paper and draw round the bottle with a pencil. Remove the bottle and neaten the lines. Add a 2.5cm (1in) seam allowance round the whole shape. When you are adding the seam allowance round the narrow parts of the neckline, soften the curves as this will make is slightly looser, and therefore easier to remove the hot water bottle from the case. Make a second copy of this template and mark a horizontal line approximately 15cm (6in) down from the top of the bottle pattern. This will form the envelope opening to allow you to remove the bottle. Cut along this line. Add a further 3cm (1¼in) to both cut lines using additional pattern paper; these will form the overlap of the opening.

2 Lay all three pattern pieces onto the fabric side of the fur, paying attention to fur direction and any animal markings. Chalk round the templates and cut out using a scalpel. Cut out two bias strips of lining each 8cm (3¼in) wide and 30cm (11¾in) long. Press in half lengthways. Pin the folded edge of the bias along each straight edge of the fur (the envelope openings). As you are doing this, place 50cm (19¾in) of the satin ribbon in the middle of each piece (the length of the ribbon should be running away from this edge). Machine stitch into place using a large stitch 5mm (¼in) away from the raw edge, combing the fur towards the centre as you stitch. To complete these sections, 'roll' the fur by folding the bias tape towards the fabric side of the fur and hand sew into position (see page 6).

3 Before assembling the main body of the case, hand sew the grosgrain ribbon to form a loop at the top. The loop should face away from the raw edge to be the right way round when turned through.

4 Now assemble the case. Pin the smaller flap to the bottle shape first and the overlap with the second flap. Match all of the edges and machine stitch closed using a large stitch, combing the fur as you stitch (see page 6) 5mm (¼in) away from the raw edge. Turn the case the right way out and insert the bottle to check fit. Fold the ribbon ends three times at 5mm (¼in) intervals and sew down to secure. Tie the ribbon in a bow.

Jacket Collar

Materials:

Faux fur tan short-haired fox fur

0.5m (19¾in) of lining fabric

One jacket/coat to trim

Tools:

Fabric scissors

Scalpel

Thread

Sewing machine

Hand sewing needles

Chalk/pencil

Long, strong pins

Ruler, tape measure and set square

Iron

Pattern paper and small weights

Tracing wheel

Instructions:

1 First, make a half pattern using the jacket. Lay out some pattern paper on a flat surface. Before drawing on the paper, take the jacket and bring both sides of the collar together. With a pin or chalk, mark the centre point at the back of the neck (called the centre back). To create the half pattern, lay the collar flat on the pattern paper (add some small weights to keep it in position) and draw round the outside. The collar should be face up as you do so. Start marking at the neck and continue along until you are level with the top of the buttonhole. Using a tracing wheel, run along the collar crease, which will be parallel to the line you have just drawn. Stop at the neck point and square off to make a centre back line.

2 Remove the jacket and fill in the tracing wheel dots with a pencil line. With a set square, square off horizontally at the buttonhole position 4cm (1½in) inwards. We are going to create a shawl collar. From the centre back line add 2cm (¾in) along the outside and inside lines. These lines should be brought down to nothing when they reach the buttonhole point. Mark an arrow pointing away from the centre back line to indicate fur direction. Cut the pattern out and use it to mark out your chosen fur, taking into account fur direction, left and right sections and adding a 5mm (¼in) seam allowance round the entire piece.

3 Bring the two fur sections together to form the centre back of the collar and pin. Machine sew the pieces together 5mm (¼in) away from the raw edge using a large stitch and combing back any fur as you sew. Now follow steps 4 and 5 of the Slide-through Scarf on page 17. You need to measure round the collar to determine how much tape you will need.

4 Chalk out a lining as one piece using your paper template, and mark the centre back position. Add an extra 2cm (¾in) seam allowance round the whole lining piece and cut out. Turn the whole collar flat, fur side down. Place the lining over the collar and match up the centre back and the buttonhole ends. Pin to hold. Now tuck under the raw edges of the lining round the perimeter and pin onto the bias tape 5mm (¼in) away from the edge. Take care when folding under the corners, so as not to make the lining tight. Hand sew the lining into position and remove the pins.

5 Now attach the collar to the jacket. The easiest way is to lay the fur flat, face down and then place the actual collar face down on top of that. Match up the centre back seam and pin the collar 2cm (¾in) away from the fur edge. Hand sew this outer edge into position first and then continue inwards. You could also add matching cuffs by following the same principles outlined in the Glove Trim project on page 8.

Child's Mittens

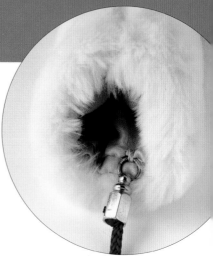

Materials:

Faux snow white short-haired
   fox fur

0.5m (19¾in) of lining fabric

1m (39½in) of red silk cord

2 x cord caps with loops

One child's hand to
   draw round

Tools:

Fabric scissors

Scalpel

Thread

Sewing machine

Hand sewing needles

Chalk/pencil

Long, strong pins

Ruler and tape measure

Iron

Pattern paper

Instructions:

1 Plot a template onto pattern paper by drawing round a child's hand with a pencil. The hand should be flat with the fingers together but the thumb extended. Start and stop at the wrist. Draw a straight line to square off at the wrist point. Add a 2cm (¾in) seam allowance round the entire piece. When you arrive between the thumb and finger area, shorten the depth of the well and soften this curve. Once you are happy with the mitten shape, cut it out. Mark an arrow pointing towards the straight wrist line to indicate the fur direction.

2 Place the pattern piece onto the fabric side of the fur and chalk four sections, two face up and two face down. Cut out with a scalpel. Match the pairs and pin together. Set a sewing machine to a large stitch and sew 5mm (¼in) away from the raw edges, leaving the wrist areas open. Repeat for both mittens. Mark out some bias strips measuring 5cm (2in) wide and about 30cm (11¾in) long on the lining fabric. Press in half lengthways. Pin the folded bias edge to the raw edge of the fur (along the opening). Overlap the bias strip back on itself at the starting point. This will achieve a nice finished edge when 'rolling' the fur. Repeat for both mittens.

3 Machine stitch along the pinned edges, combing any fur to the centre. As you reach the beginning of the stitch line, overlap the bias tape by about 4cm (1½in). Cut off any excess tape. To complete this stage of the mittens, 'roll' the fur by folding the bias tape towards the fabric side of the fur and hand sew into position (see page 6).

4 To make linings for the mittens, simply chalk out two sections with the lining fabric folded double. Before cutting out, add an extra 1cm (½in) seam allowance to both pieces. Cut out, then machine stitch the linings together using the 1cm (½in) allowance. Trim the allowance 5mm (¼in) away from the stitch line. With the iron, press under the 1cm (½in) seam allowance round the lining opening. Drop these into the fur mittens and hand sew into place, matching the side seams.

5 Cut the cord to the desired length and add the cord caps. Hand sew the metal loops to the insides of the mittens.

Teddy Hat

Materials:

Faux caramel fox fur

0.5m (19¾in) of lining fabric

Pink felt scraps

One child's head to measure

Tools:

Fabric scissors

Scalpel

Thread

Sewing machine

Hand sewing needles

Chalk/pencil

Long, strong pins

Iron

Sheet of paper, 210 x 297mm
   (8¼ x 11¾in)

Ruler, tape measure and
   set square

Instructions:

1 Making this pattern is simple. Take two measurements from the child's head, one being the circumference and the other from the front to the nape. Divide the circumference by four and the front to nape by two. Fold a sheet of paper in half lengthways. With the crease pointing towards you, mark the front to nape measurement. Now divide the circumference measurement by a further two. Mark this measurement vertically from the bottom left-hand corner. Draw a descending curved line from the left point to the right. Cut out and unfold. You now have a quarter pattern with which to make the hat.

2 Use this pattern to mark out the hat onto the fabric side of the fur with chalk. You will need to add a 1cm (½in) seam allowance round all pattern pieces. Extend two of the crown sections vertically by 80cm (31½in) to form the hat flaps. The fur direction should run away from the tip of the crown. Cut all four sections using a scalpel. Repeat this process to make a lining. Use the existing pattern to make a template for the ears. Measure along the crease line of the paper from the pointed end approximately 8cm (3¼in) and square off vertically across the crease line (you should now have a smaller version of the master pattern). Make a separate copy of the smaller version.

3 Use the new pattern to cut out two felt sections and two in fur. This time you will only need to add a 5mm (¼in) seam allowance and the fur direction should point towards the pointed part of the pattern. Pin the felt and fur sections together and machine stitch 5mm

(¼in) away from the raw edge, combing the fur inwards as you sew, and using a large stitch. Turn each piece through and pin to the outside edge of one of the smaller crown sections. Fold over part of the ear to give character and position approximately 6cm (2¼in) away from the tip of the crown.

4 Assemble all of the crown sections together and pin. The pieces should alternate in size. Make sure you match up the original circumference line. Machine sew together using a large stitch 1cm (½in) away from the raw edge. Comb the fur inwards while sewing. Repeat this process for the lining sections.

5 Cut out two bias strips of lining fabric, each 8cm (3¼in) wide and about 20cm (7¾in) long.

Press in half lengthways. Pin the folded edge of the bias along each straight edge of the fur (the base of the smaller crown sections of the hat). Machine stitch into place using a large stitch 5mm (¼in) away from the raw edge, combing the fur towards the centre as you stitch. To complete these sections, 'roll' the fur by folding the bias tape towards the fabric side of the fur and hand sew into position (see page 6).

6 Pin the made-up lining shell onto the fur. Match the seams. Machine stitch as above, but only the flap sections. Start and stop stitching at the circumference line. Turn the flaps through. Invert the crown lining into position. Turn over 1cm (½in) seam allowance along the opening and hand sew closed onto the bias strips.

Beaded Evening Bag

Materials:

Faux black mink fur

0.5m (19¾in) of lining fabric

2m (78¾in) of silk braid

Approx. 40 black crystals (20 per side)

4 x eyelets

Thread

Sewing machine

Hand sewing needles

Chalk/pencil

Long, strong pins

Ruler, tape measure and set square

Iron

Sheet of paper, 210 x 297mm (8¼ x 11¾in)

Tools:

Fabric scissors

Scalpel

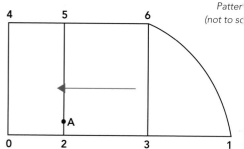

Instructions:

1 Take a sheet of paper and fold it in half lengthways. With the crease pointing towards you, plot out the following along the crease line: 0–1 = 25cm (9¾in), 0–2 = 8cm (3¼in), 0–3 =15cm (6in), 0–4 = 10cm (4in), 4–5 = 8cm (3¼in), and 4–6 = 15cm (6in). Join 6–1 with a descending curve. 'A' is an eyelet position and should be marked 1.5cm (⁵/₈in) away from '2'. Cut out and unfold the paper. 'Mirror' all of the drawn information on the blank side now exposed. The fur direction should point away for the round section of the pattern.

2 Mark out four sections onto the fabric side of the fur. Transfer all appropriate information. You will only need to mark the eyelet position on two sections. Do not add any seam allowance and cut out using a scalpel. Attach each eyelet following the manufacturer's instructions. Hand sew approximately 20 crystals onto the fur side of each section in a random fashion. Pin together all of the sections of the fur along the raw edges, matching up the casing lines. Machine sew along each seam 1cm (½in) away from the raw edges, combing the fur inwards as you sew.

3 Cut out a section of lining measuring 8 x 80cm (3¼ x 31½in). Press the whole strip lengthways. Now pin the centre of this strip along the casing line. Overlap the starting point to finish. Hand sew the lining edge which

is furthest away from the opening and remove the pins. Cut the silk braid in half. From the fur side, insert one end of the braid and bring it round the whole bag to come back through the adjoining eyelet. Repeat the process on the other side. Sandwich the braids into the casing and hand sew it closed, trapping the braids within. Tie the corresponding braids together and fray the edges to form tassels.

4 Chalk out a further four sections onto the lining fabric to form the bag lining. At the same time, cut a long bias strip 8cm (3¼in) wide and approximately 80cm (31½in) long. Press in half lengthways. Pin the folded edge to the rim of the bag and pin. Overlap the bias strip back on itself at the starting point. This will achieve a nice finished edge when 'rolling' the fur.

Patter (not to sc

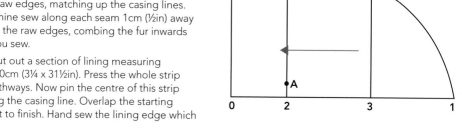

5 Machine stitch with a large stitch along the bias tape 5mm (¼in) away from the raw edge, combing any fur towards the centre as you sew. When you reach the beginning of the stitch line overlap the bias tape by about 4cm (1½in). Cut off any excess tape. To complete this stage of the bag, 'roll' the fur by folding the bias tape towards the fabric side of the fur and hand sew into position (see page 6).

6 Machine stitch the lining sections together using a 1cm (½in) seam allowance. After sewing, press under the 1cm (½in) seam allowance round the rim of the piece with an iron. Drop the lining into the bag and pin to hold, matching up the seams. Hand sew the lining to the bias tape to secure.

Cosy Muff

Materials:

Faux chocolate short-haired fox fur

0.5m (19¾in) of lining fabric

0.5m (19¾in) of fleece

2m (78¾in) of silk braid

Collar/bridal canvas 20 x 80cm (7¾in x 31½)

Black elastic 0.4cm x 15cm (³/₁₆ x 6in)

Tools:

Fabric scissors

Scalpel

Thread

Sewing machine

Hand sewing needles

Chalk/pencil

Long, strong pins

Ruler, tape measure and set square

Iron

Sheets of paper, 210 x 297mm (8¼ x 11¾in)

Sticky tape

Instructions:

1 Join two sheets of paper with sticky tape along one of the long edges. Fold together with the sticky tape inside. With the taped edge facing you, plot onto this line the following (using the diagram opposite): 1–2 = 24.5cm (9⁵/₈in), 1–3 = 18cm (7in), 3–4 = 24.5 (9⁵/₈in), 2–4 = 18cm (7in) then 1–5 = 6cm (2¼in), 2–6 = 6cm (2¼in). Join 5–6. 5–A = 6cm (2¼in) and 6–B = 6cm (2¼in), then 3–7 = 1.5cm (⁵/₈in), 7–8 = 3cm (1¼in), 8–9 = 3cm (1¼in), 4–12 = 1.5cm (⁵/₈in), 12–11 = 3cm (1¼in) and 11–10 = 3cm (1¼in). Join 8–9 with A, 10–11 with B, 7–5 and 12–6. Cut the template out and unfold the paper.

2 Place the template onto the fabric side of the fur and chalk out three sections, paying attention to the fur direction. Do not add any seam allowance. Cut out with a scalpel. Repeat this process with the fleece to form a lining. Pin all of the darts closed and machine close 5mm (¼in) away from the raw edges. Repeat this for all three sections in fur, and then again with the fleece. Now pin the three fur sections together. Make sure the fur is running in the same direction and sew along the seam 1cm (½in) away from the raw edge, combing any fur inwards as you sew. Repeat to complete the fleece lining in the same way.

3 Place the collar canvas onto the fabric side of the fur symmetrically round the barrel-like shape. Secure this to the muff by hand sewing a large stitch running through the centre of the canvas. Slightly clip into the canvas (inwards) round the edge of the tube. Flatten the snipped sections down onto the muff and lightly hand sew to secure, following the barrel shape of the muff.

4 Cut two bias strips 8cm (3¼in) wide and about 50cm (19¾in) long of the lining fabric. Press in half lengthways. Pin each strip with the folded edge to the rim of the muff. Overlap the bias strip back on itself at the starting point. This will achieve a finished edge when 'rolling' the fur.

5 Machine stitch with a large stitch along the bias tape 5mm (¼in) away from the raw edge, combing any fur towards the centre as you sew. As you reach the beginning of the stitch line, overlap the bias tape by approximately 4cm (1½in). Cut off any excess tape. To complete this stage of the muff, 'roll' the fur by folding the bias tape towards the fabric side of the fur and hand sew into position (see page 6).

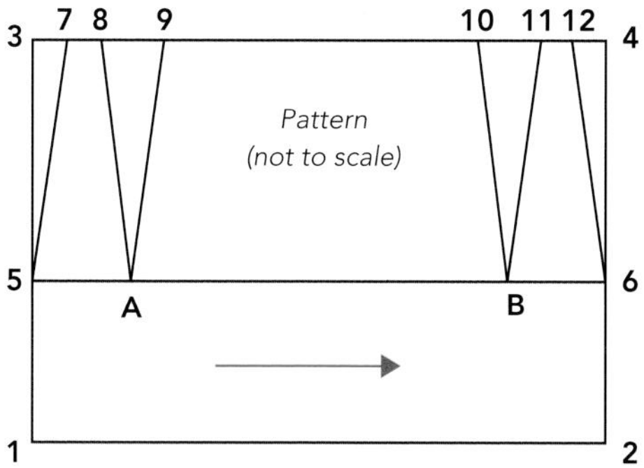
3
7
8
9
10
11
12
4
Pattern
(not to scale)
5
A
B
6
1
2

6 Position an elastic loop either side of one of the muff's seams. Fold over a 7.5cm (3in) length of elastic to form a loop and secure tightly to the inside of the muff's rim with the loop facing out. Pull over the fleece lining and pin to hold, matching the seam. Fold under 1cm (½in) round the rim and hand sew into position. Pull the muff through. Tie large knots at the ends of the braid and insert into the loops to form the neck cord.

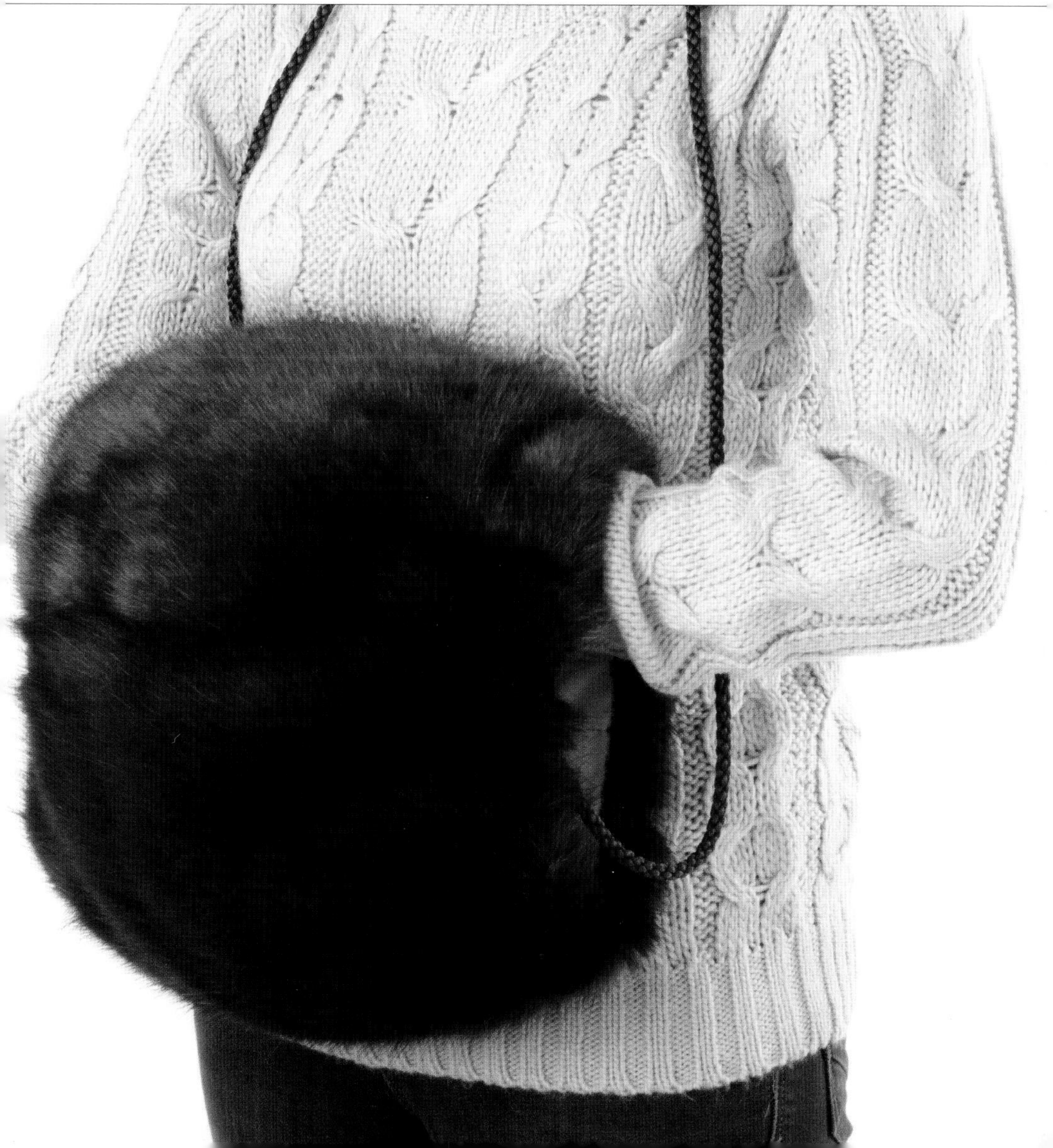

Heart Pillow

Materials:

1m square (39½in sq) faux
  shocking pink fun fur

1m (39½in) pink felt lining, as
  wide as possible

1m square (39½in sq) doubled
  over cotton

Beanbag balls

Sew-on hook and
  loop fastening

Tools:

Fabric scissors

Scalpel

Thread

Sewing machine

Hand sewing needles

Chalk/pencil

Long, strong pins

Ruler and tape measure

Pattern paper

Instructions:

1 Fold in half a piece of pattern paper
measuring 1m (39½in) square. Using the crease
as a central line, draw half of a heart shape,
filling the space on the remaining paper.
Once you are happy with the shape, cut it out
and unfold. Use this heart shape to chalk out
one section in fur and two in cotton. The fur
direction should be running towards the point
of the heart. Cut out the pieces with a scalpel.

2 Find the crease line on the paper pattern
and plot a line running parallel 15cm (6in) away
towards the right with the heart facing towards
you. Cut the heart in two along the new line. Lay
these new pieces onto the pink felt and chalk
round the perimeter. When marking out the
larger piece, add an extra 15cm (6in) onto the
straight line to form an overlap. This will create
an envelope opening for stuffing the pillow. Cut
out the pieces with scissors.

3 Fold under a 1cm (½in) seam allowance
and top stitch the felt with a sewing machine
to secure. Now place the heart fur side up on
a table top. Layer the smaller felt piece face
down, followed by the larger piece, matching

all of the curves as you position them. Pin to
secure. Sew with a large stitch, machining the
felt and fur together 1cm (½in) away from the
raw edge, combing any protruding fur inwards
as you sew. Pull through and add the hook and
loop fastening along the envelope opening.
Hand sew to secure.

4 Sew the cotton heart together using a 1cm
(½in) seam allowance. On one of the heart
sides leave an opening of about 20cm (7¾in) to
allow stuffing. Turn the heart through and stuff
with the balls. Do this carefully: using the neck
of the bag in which the balls are contained, slip
this into the opening and pour the balls in –
otherwise it can be a very messy job.

5 Fill the cotton heart approximately three-
quarters full and close the opening. Place this
into the furry outer case and close.

Draught Excluder

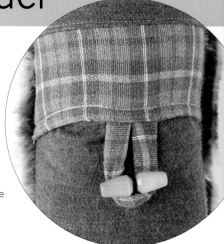

Materials:

20 x 90cm (7¾ x 35½in) faux chocolate chinchilla fur

Wool fabric for backing

Scraps of checked wool fabric for overlap and toggle loop

Toy stuffing

1 x wooden toggle

Tools:

Fabric scissors

Scalpel

Thread

Sewing machine

Hand sewing needles

Chalk/pencil

Long, strong pins

Ruler and tape measure

Iron

Instructions:

1 This draught excluder is made using one rectangle in fur and two in a wool fabric. Start by chalking out a long rectangle in fur measuring 20 x 90cm (7¾in x 35½). Add a 1cm (½in) seam allowance round the whole piece. Make sure that the fur direction is running vertical to the long edge of the rectangle. Cut out with a scalpel and place to one side.

2 Lay the wool fabric flat and chalk out two rectangles measuring 20 x 45cm (7¾ x 17¾in). Add a 1cm (½in) seam allowance round each piece and cut out. Next, lay out the checked wool and chalk out two sections measuring 6 x 20cm (2¼ x 7¾in), adding a 1cm (½in) seam allowance. Chalk a further strip measuring 4 x 20cm (1½ x 7¾in). Cut all three out. Using the 4cm (1½in) wide strip, fold in half lengthways (right sides together) and machine sew 1cm (½in) away from the raw edge. Turn this strip through to reveal a tube. This will form the loop (see above).

3 With right sides facing, lay the remaining checked pieces together. Pin along one of the 20cm (7¾in) long sides inserting the loop so that it is sandwiched in the middle. Machine close using a 1cm (½in) seam allowance. Pull the loose sections back on themselves to reveal the loop and press along the seam edge. Top stitch along the pressed edge to hold in place. Attach the remaining 20cm (7¾in) checked edge to one of the wool sections, machine as before, then press and top stitch to complete.

4 With the fur side facing you, layer the looped section on top followed by the remaining wool section. Match up the four corners and then pin towards the centre. Now sew round the perimeter using a 1cm (½in) seam allowance. Use a large machine stitch (size 4–5) and sew up the piece, making sure you comb any protruding fur inwards.

5 Turn through and stuff with the toy stuffing. Finally, hand sew the wooden toggle onto the rear so that the loop fits round it.

Scatter Pillow

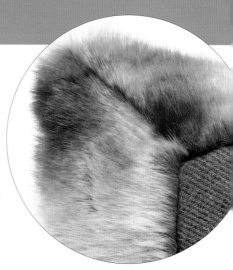

Materials:

Faux chocolate chinchilla fur

1m (39½in) of backing fabric

4 x checked tweeds, each
    11 x 11cm (4¼ x 4¼ in)

Toy stuffing or a made-
    to-measure pillow pad
    Finished pillow measures
    38 x 38cm (15 x 15in)

Tools:

Fabric scissors

Scalpel

Thread

Sewing machine

Chalk

Long, strong pins

Ruler, tape measure
    and set square

Iron

Instructions:

1 Start by sewing the four squares of tweed together using a 1cm (½in) seam allowance. Press the seams flat at the rear with a hot iron and place to one side. Lay out the backing fabric and cut out two squares measuring 40 x 40cm (15¾ x 15¾in). Fold over 15cm (6in) along one side of the first square and press. Repeat this process for the other square and put to one side.

2 Chalk out strips directly onto the fabric side of the fur with a depth of 9cm (3½in) and 38cm (15in) in length horizontally. With a set square, mitre the corners. The shorter line should measure 20cm (7¾in) in length and the longer 38cm (15in). Now add a 1cm (½in) seam allowance round all edges. You need four strips in total. The fur direction should run away from the shorter horizontal line. Cut out using a scalpel.

3 Line up the short edges of the fur strips along the four edges of the tweed. Pin and machine sew into position with a large stitch, combing any stray fur inwards as you sew. Complete all four edges. Pin the mitred corners and stitch them closed in the same manner.

4 Place the fur-trimmed tweed facing up and layer over the backing pieces. The first piece should be laid with the pressed edge facing you and resting over the middle of the pillow. Match up the outer corners and pin. Add the second backing section likewise. Machine stitch the entire pillow round the perimeter using a 1cm (½in) seam allowance, combing the fur as you stitch. Pull the work through and fill the pillow with toy stuffing or a pillow pad.

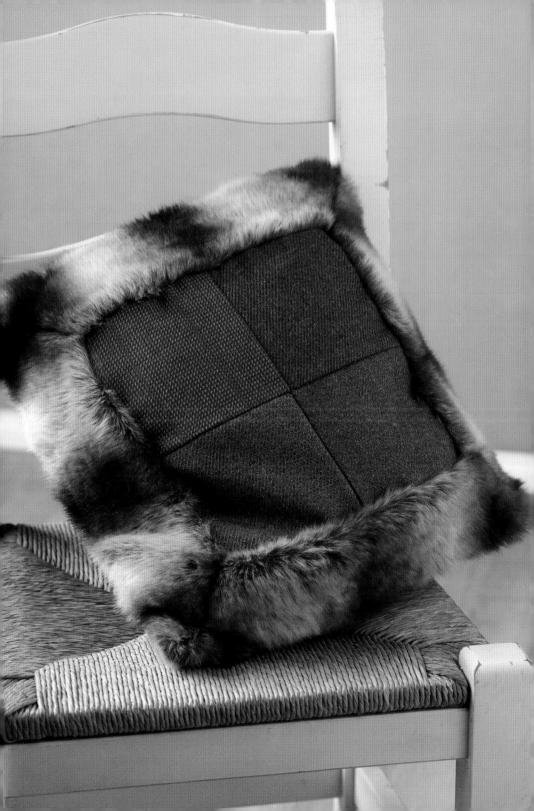

Earmuffs

Materials:

Faux silver chinchilla fur

Black velvet

2 x small round sponges approx. 9cm (3½in)across 4.5cm (1¾in) high

2.5cm (1in) wide plastic hairband

Scraps of black felt

Tools:

Fabric scissors

Scalpel

Thread (strong and normal)

Sewing machine

Hand sewing needles: long and short

Chalk/pencil

Long, strong pins

Ruler and tape measure

Sheet of paper, 210 x 297mm (8¼ x 11¾in)

Glue gun

Pattern paper

Compasses

Instructions:

1 Plot out the following onto a sheet of paper: 0–1 = 21cm (8¼in), 0–4 = 3cm (1¼in), 0–5 = 3cm (1in), 1–2 = 1.5cm (½in) and 1–3 = 1.5cm (½in). Join 4–5 and 5–3. Now add a 1cm (½in) seam allowance round the whole piece and cut out. Mark round this pattern twice onto the back of the black velvet with chalk and cut out. For each piece, bring the longer edges of the velvet together and pin to hold. Machine stitch 1cm (½in) away from the raw edge. Flatten out the seam allowance towards the smaller opening and position to run along the centre of the piece. Machine the opening closed and trim back 5mm (¼in) away from the stitch line. Pull through and insert the hairband. The seam should be on the underside of the band. Repeat with the second piece to cover the hairband. Bring the top ends together, hand stitching to secure them. Cover this join with another strip of velvet. Hide the raw edges by turning under and sewing directly to the band.

2 Set a compass to 10cm (4in), draw a circle onto pattern paper and cut out. Mark out two circles using the template and chalk onto the reverse of the fur. Cut out using a scalpel. With a very strong thread, apply a running stitch round the perimeter of each circle 5mm (¼in) away from the raw edge, leaving the thread ends free. Draw both threads together at the same time to encase the sponge and form the earmuff. Tie a series of knots to secure the fur round the sponge. Hide the thread ends inside the earmuff.

3 Position the ends of the headband to the inside of the earmuff over the drawn opening. With a long needle and strong thread sew the end onto the earmuff. Sew directly through the earmuff and catch the velvet round the band for best results.

4 Cut out two circles of felt with a diameter of 5cm (2in). Lay each one onto the back of some velvet and cut 1cm (½in) away from the felt edge. Place a running stitch round the velvet edge and pull it over the felt disc in the same way the fur encased the sponge. Secure the threads at the rear. To finish, attach the disc to the centre of the earmuff using a glue gun, trapping the end of the hairband under the felt and velvet disc.

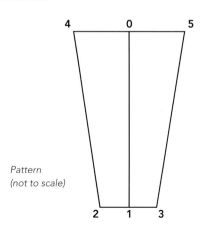

*Pattern
(not to scale)*

Headband

Materials:

Faux silver fox fur

Black lining fabric

Good-quality black felt

Black elastic, 2cm (¾in) wide

Tools:

Fabric scissors

Scalpel

Thread (strong and normal)

Sewing machine

Hand sewing needles

Chalk/pencil

Long, strong pins

Ruler and tape measure

Pattern paper

Iron

Instructions:

1 Measure the circumference of your head. Draw a horizontal line onto some pattern paper and mark this measurement. Measure and draw in a depth of 7cm (2¾in). You should now be looking at a rectangular shape. Shorten this rectangular shape by 8cm (3¼in) to create two shapes, then cut them both out.

2 Use these pattern pieces and chalk the shapes onto the fabric side of the fur, horizontal to the fur's vertical flow. Add a 5mm (¼in) seam allowance to all sides and cut out using a scalpel. Now turn to page 8 and follow steps 3–4 of the Glove Trim project. Do not join the fur sections together. You will need to cut enough bias tape from the black lining fabric to trim round every side of both pieces of fur.

3 With the fur 'rolled', bridge together the sections of the headband by laying over two strips of elastic horizontally across the finished vertical edges. Match the corners and hand sew the elastic securely into place. The headband should be in one piece now.

4 Lay the pattern pieces onto the felt and chalk round. Reduce the pieces by 5mm (¼in) round each edge and cut out. Lay the corresponding felt strips onto the reverse of the fur to act as a lining. Hand stitch to finish. The felt will help hold the band on your head, whereas lining material would allow the band to slip off. The elastic sections will allow the band to move with your head.

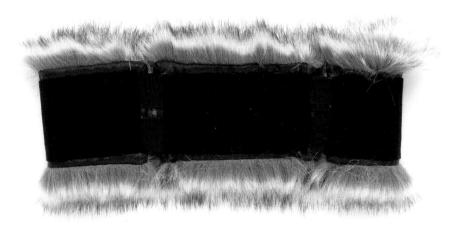

Monster Beanbag

Materials:

Green shaggy faux fur (10cm/4in pile):
  100 x 160cm (39½ x 63in) and 50 x 160cm
  (19¾ x 63in)

Purple and blue felt, extra wide

Toy stuffing

46cm (18in) zip

Cotton to line beanbag, 100 x 160cm
  (39½ x 63in)

Beanbag balls

Tools:

Fabric scissors

Scalpel

Thread

Sewing machine

Chalk/pencil

Long, strong pins

Ruler and tape measure

Pattern paper

Pushpin and string

Instructions:

1 Draw a circle measuring 52cm (20½in) in diameter on a large sheet of pattern paper. To do this, make a loop in some string and insert a pencil into the loop. Measure down from the loop to 26cm (10¼in). This will give you a radius. Secure the end of the string to the pattern paper with a pushpin and draw the circle. The pin will allow the string and pencil to pivot round. Cut out the circle, then fold and cut the circle in half. Use one half of the paper pattern to mark out two sections onto the blue felt. Add a 1cm (½in) seam allowance along the straight edge and set aside. Make a copy of the pattern piece onto pattern paper and draw in some feet, using the diagram below as a guide. Cut out.

2 Mark out two sections of purple felt to measure 50 x 150cm (19¾ x 59in) and cut out. Fold and pin in half lengthways. With the crease of the felt facing away from you, draw in a length of spikes that will run along the tail (see the diagram below for guidance). Mark out four feet sections with chalk onto the same coloured felt and cut out. Divide into pairs and pin. Machine stitch the feet and spiky backbone 1cm (½in) away from the raw edges. Clip into the seam allowance, snipping into the corners and across the

points. Turn both sections through and stuff the points and feet with toy stuffing. Machine close the opening.

3 Cut out another piece of pattern paper measuring 50 x 150cm (19¾ x 59in). Fold the piece lengthways. With the crease facing you, draw out a curved tail following the diagram below. Cut out and unfold. Lay this onto the reverse of the green fur and mark out with chalk. Cut out with a scalpel. Pin one of the fur edges to the raw edge of the felt backbone and machine down into place. Comb the fur inwards as you stitch. Repeat this process to trap the spikes into the fur. Turn through and stuff with toy stuffing.

4 To make the monster body, measure a fur rectangle 100 x 160cm (39½ x 63in) in green fur. Bring the shorter edges together and pin. With the fur folded, round off the top of the rectangle as shown below freehand. Pin or baste the tail into the bottom section of the

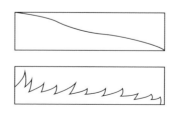

Pattern (not to scale)

body along the seam allowance. Machine stitch using a large stitch round the curved chalk line and down the straight edge. Do not cut anything off. Take extra care at the tail section and comb the fur inwards as you sew.

5 Attach the zip between the two straight edges of the blue felt circle and top stitch down to strengthen. Pin the circle to the base of the green fur body. Sandwich the feet between these layers. Make sure the feet are pointing in the right direction. Sew round the entire circumference of the base as above. Turn the beanbag through.

6 Fold the cotton fabric in half and sew together, leaving an opening to allow stuffing – essentially, this is a giant pillowcase. Turn through and fill approximately two-thirds full with beanbag balls. Do this carefully: using the neck of the bag in which the balls are contained, slip this into the opening and pour the balls in – otherwise it can be a very messy job. Close the pillow by machining the opening closed. Stuff the monster beanbag with the pillow and zip it up to finish.

Bolero

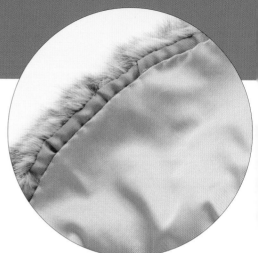

Materials:

Faux jaguar mink fur

1.5m (59in) of lining fabric

One old, loose-fitting, crew-neck T-shirt

Tools:

Fabric scissors

Scalpel

Thread

Sewing machine

Chalk/pencil

Long, strong pins

Ruler and tape measure

Pattern paper

Iron

Instructions:

1 First, try the T-shirt on and, using a mirror, decide where you wish the gilet to finish under the arm. Use the diagrams below as a guide. Lay the T-shirt onto a flat surface and draw a curved line with a pencil from the top of the neckline down to the side seam (see below left). This will need to be done freehand to achieve a flowing line. Flip the T-shirt over and draw in the back curve to meet the centre back (see below right). You should now have marked a half pattern. With fabric scissors, cut out along your marked lines. Cut along the shoulder line, side seam and round the armhole until you have three flat pattern pieces.

2 Lay these pieces on the pattern paper and mark round them with a pencil. Remove the cloth pieces and neaten the lines. Make sure you flip the back section over and mirror the information towards the other side, plotting a whole back pattern.

3 With the fur side down, use the pattern pieces to mark out two front sections, two armholes and one back. Make sure you pay attention to any animal markings and fur direction (see the arrows on the diagrams) as you lay the pieces out, so that they match. Be very patient when laying out, for the best results. Add a 1cm (½in) seam allowance round all sections and cut out with a scalpel. Pin the front sections to the back via the shoulder line and side seams. Machine together using a large stitch 1cm (½in) away from the raw edges. Comb the fur inwards as you sew. Using the same method, sew the sleeves together and attach to the main body.

4 Turn to page 8 and follow steps 3–4 of the Glove Trim project. Measure round the arms and the gilet body to determine the length required. You may have to stitch bias strips together to obtain the correct length.

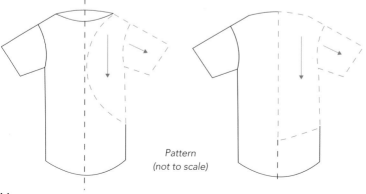

*Pattern
(not to scale)*

5 To line the gilet, use the pattern pieces to mark and cut out a second gilet from the lining fabric; however, this time add a 1.5cm (⅝in) seam allowance round every section. This will give some ease to the lining. As above, machine stitch the lining together using a 1cm (½in) seam allowance. Offer the lining to the gilet and pin. Match up the centre back, side seam and armhole points. Turn under the raw edges of the seam allowance and hand stitch onto the bias tape 5mm (¼in) away from the fur edge.

Christmas Stocking

Materials:

Faux cream fox fur

1m (39½in) of red
   silk dupion

30cm (11¾in) of white
   cord for the loop

Tools:

Fabric scissors

Scalpel

Thread

Sewing machine

Chalk/pencil

Long, strong pins

Ruler and tape measure

Pattern paper

Iron

Instructions:

1 Cut out a piece of pattern paper 40 x 60cm (15¾ x 23½in). Draw a stocking shape to fill the paper and cut out. Lay this pattern piece onto the red silk dupion. Mark out two stockings for this pattern and cut out. You should have four pieces. Pin together in pairs with right sides together and machine stitch round the outer edge 1cm (½in) away from the raw edge. Clip into the curved areas of the seam allowance to help produce a better shape when turned through. Repeat for both stockings.

2 Turn one stocking through and place the other directly into it to act as a lining. Match up the side seams and the rims of the stocking tops. Turn over and press under a 1cm (½in) seam allowance onto the outer shell of the stocking. Put to one side.

3 Measure the circumference of the stocking top. With chalk, plot the measurement directly onto the fabric side of the fur with a horizontal line, with the fur direction running vertically to this. Square down to give a depth of 8cm (3¼in) at both ends of your marked line. Join these points horizontally to create a rectangle shape. Add a 5mm (¼in) seam allowance round the whole shape and cut out using a scalpel. Bring the short ends of each section together and pin to secure. Machine stitch 5mm (¼in) away from the raw edge using a large stitch. As you stitch, comb any fur towards the centre of the piece (see page 6).

4 Lay the lining flat and chalk out some bias strips 8cm (3¼in) wide and about 10cm (4in) longer than the circumference measurement. You will need two strips. Cut them out. Press each piece in half along the longest edge. Take the fur band and pin the folded bias edge to the raw edge of the fur. Overlap the bias strip back on itself at the starting point. This will achieve a nice finished edge when 'rolling' the fur. Repeat on the other side.

5 Machine stitch (size 4–5) along the pinned edges, combing any fur to the centre. As you reach the beginning of the stitch line, overlap the bias tape by approximately 4cm (1½in). Cut off any excess tape. To complete the fur band, 'roll' the fur by folding the bias tape towards the fabric side of the fur and hand sew into position (see page 6).

6 Turn the fur band to the fur side and slip over the rim of the stocking. Match up the back seam and pin to hold. Fold the cord in two and tie a knot to secure the ends. Insert this knot between the fur and the stocking. Hand sew the fur band into place along the rim of the stocking 5mm (¼in) away from the fur edge, trapping the cord within.

Acknowledgements

Alistair would like to thank the team at Search Press, including May Corfield for her editorial support, Paul Bricknell for the beautiful photography and Juan Hayward and Marrianne Miall for the beautiful staging and styling. Also, a special thank you to everyone supporting me by buying a copy of my furry book – I hope you enjoy it!

Publisher's Note
You are invited to visit the author's website:
www.houseofalistair.com